World in Focus
Sweden

NICOLA BARBER

WAYLAND

First published in 2007 by Wayland

Wayland
338 Euston Road, London NW1 3BH

Wayland Australia
Hachette Children's Books
Level 17/207 Kent Street
Sydney, NSW 2000

Commissioning editor: Nicola Edwards
Editor: Patience Coster
Inside design: Chris Halls, www.mindseyedesign.co.uk
Cover design: Wayland
Series concept and project management by EASI-Educational Resourcing
(info@easi-er.co.uk)
Statistical research: Anna Bowden
Maps and graphs: Martin Darlison, Encompass Graphics

Printed and bound in China

British Library Cataloguing in Publication Data
Barber, Nicola
   Sweden. - (World in focus)
   1. Sweden - Juvenile literature
   I. Title
   948.5'06

ISBN-13: 9780750247412
ISBN-10: 075024741X

Cover top: Kalmar Slott (Kalmar Castle), site of the proclamation of the Kalmar Union.
Cover bottom: The Ice Hotel in Jukkasjärvi is made every year from the crystal-clear frozen waters of the Torne River.
Title page: A hiker sits on a rock above the Rapa River valley in Sarek National Park, northern Sweden.

The author and publisher would like to thank the following for allowing their pictures to be reproduced in this publication:
Alamy 20 (Nordicphotos), 27 (Pixonnet.com), 29 (Bjorn Svensson), 40 (Frank Chmura), 42 (Chad Ehlers), 44 (Stock
Connection Distribution), 56 (Martin Bond); Corbis 4 (Hans Strand), 6 (Wolfgang Rattay/Reuters), 9 (Macduff Everton),
10 (Macduff Everton), *cover (top)* and 11 (Macduff Everton), 12 (The Art Archive), 13 (Peter Turnley), 14 (Hubert Stadler),
16 (Jorma Jaemsen/Zefa), 17 (Anders Ryman), 19 (Bo Zaunders), 21 (Fridmar Damm/Zefa), 25 (Steve Raymer), 28
(Alexander Benz/Zefa), 31 (Frederic Pitchal), 33 (Steve Raymer), 35 (Hulton-Deutsch Collection), 37 (Stefan Lindblom),
43 (Anders Ryman), 45 (Zwalm dan Vander), 46 (Historical Picture Archive), 47 (Denis O'Regan), 49 (Anders Ryman),
title page and 50 (Hans Strand), 51 (Tony Gentile/Reuters), 52 (US Air Force), *cover (bottom)* and 53 (Hans Strand), 54
(Staffan Widstrand), 59 (Blaine Harrington III); Corbis Sygma 24 (Lena Ulvenstam); EASI-Images (Rob Bowden) 38; EASI-
Images (Edward Parker) 5, 8, 15, 18, 22, 23, 26, 30, 32, 34, 36, 39, 41, 48, 55, 57, 58.

The directional arrow portrayed on the map on page 7 provides only an approximation of north.
The data used to produce the graphics and data panels in this title were the latest available at the time of production.

CONTENTS

CHAPTER 1

Sweden –
An Overview

Sweden is part of Scandinavia, the group of northern European countries that also includes Norway and Denmark. It is the largest Scandinavian country, and is very prosperous, with high standards of living. The Swedes are extremely proud of their beautiful country, with its vast areas of unspoilt landscape, its beautiful coastline, its rich natural resources and long history.

Sweden is a long, thin country which extends north beyond the Arctic Circle. This means that in its northernmost regions there is 24-hour darkness for a period during the winter and 24-hour sunlight at midsummer (see page 15). Its landscapes include the dramatic mountain ranges of the north-west, extensive forests and lakes, the rocky coastline of the west and the wide plains of the south. The Swedes love outdoor activities, and make great use of the natural attractions of their country. Fishing, skiing and cycling are among some of the most popular outdoor pursuits.

▼ Children play under a sea stack in Fårö, Sweden, a small island to the north of Gotland in the Baltic Sea. Sea stacks such as these have been carved out of the soft limestone rock by the wind and waves.

SWEDEN AND ITS NEIGHBOURS

Sweden has close ties with its nearest neighbours Norway, Finland and Denmark. It shares land borders with both Norway and Finland, and the narrow sea strait between Denmark and Sweden has recently been crossed by the Öresund Link (see page 39). The history of the four nations is closely intertwined – Sweden, Norway and Denmark were united under one monarch in 1397 (see page 10), and Finland was part of Sweden until 1809. Norway was united once again with Sweden during the nineteenth century (see page 12), until its independence in 1905.

SWEDEN'S CITIES

The vast majority of the Swedish population lives in the southern part of the country, and it is here that the biggest cities are located. Sweden's capital is the beautiful city of Stockholm, situated on an archipelago on the Baltic coast (see page 21). The second biggest city in Sweden is Göteborg on the west coast. Nicknamed by its residents the 'face of Sweden', it has long acted as a gateway to Sweden for the outside world. It is a major industrial city and home to the Swedish car manufacturer Volvo. The third biggest city, Malmö, is on the south coast. Like both Stockholm and Göteborg, Malmö is a major port with many high-tech industries, for example, ones specializing in information technology. The opening of the Öresund Link between Malmö and Copenhagen in 2000 was a major landmark in the city's history.

? Did you know?

The Swedish national anthem celebrates the beauty of the country, hailing Sweden as the 'loveliest land on the earth'.

▼ This aerial view of Sweden's capital, Stockholm, is taken from the Kaknäs Television Tower.

A DEMOCRATIC NATION

Sweden is a parliamentary democracy, with a monarch as its head of state. Since 1917, the monarch has had no real political power (although this was not formalized until 1974), but he or she is considered to be important as a representative for Sweden, and the royal family is very popular. Democracy and equality are extremely important principles in Sweden. Great emphasis has been laid on equality between men and women in Swedish society. There is a high proportion of women in the Swedish parliament (see page 23), and the welfare state provides generous support to allow both men and women to work after the birth of a child. Sweden's welfare state, which covers areas such as healthcare, education, childcare, pensions and care of the elderly, is one of the most extensive in the world. It is paid for by high taxes (see page 25), but most Swedes are proud of the way their country takes care of all of its people according to their needs.

Physical geography

- Land area: 410,934 sq km/ 158,662 sq miles
- Water area: 39,030 sq km/15,069 sq miles
- Total area: 449,964 sq km/173,731 sq miles
- World rank (by area): 55
- Land boundaries: 2,233 km/1,388 miles
- Border countries: Finland, Norway
- Coastline: 3,218 km/2,000 miles
- Highest point: Kebnekaise (2,111 m/6,926 ft)
- Lowest point: reclaimed bay of Lake Hammarsjon, near Kristianstad (-2.41 m / -7.9 ft)

Source: CIA World Factbook

Focus on: Sweden's national day

Since 2005, Sweden's national day, 6 June, has been declared a public holiday. This date was chosen as a national day for two reasons: it was the day in 1523 when Gustav Vasa was elected king of Sweden (see page 11), and in 1809 it was the day on which Sweden adopted a new constitution. National day has been celebrated every year since 1916.

? Did you know?

The design of the Swedish flag dates from the sixteenth century. Its design is probably taken from the Danish flag.

◀ Members of the Swedish royal family arrive for the Nobel Dinner (see page 37) in Stockholm in 2004. On the left is Crown Princess Victoria, heir to the throne, and on the right is her younger brother Prince Carl Philip. They are escorting their great aunt, Princess Lilian.

North
Sea

NORWAY

FINLAND

ESTONIA

LATVIA

LITHUANIA

KALININGRAD
(RUSSIAN FED)

DENMARK

GERMANY

POLAND

Baltic Sea

Gulf of
Bothnia

Kattegat

0   100   200 kilometres
0   100   200 miles

Legend
★ Capital
● Cities > 100,000
● Cities > 50,000
• other cities
▲ Mountain

KÖLEN MOUNTAINS

Kebnekaise
2,111m
Kiruna
LAPPLAND

NORRBOTTEN
Jokkmokk

Haparanda
Arvidsjaur
Piteå   Luleå

NORRLAND
VÄSTERBOTTEN
Skellefteå

SWEDEN

Umeå

VÄSTER-
NORRLAND
Östersund
Örnsköldsvik

JÄMTLAND

Sundsvall

GÄVLEBORG

DALARNA

Falun   Gävle
Borlänge
UPPSALA
SVEALAND
VÄSTMANLAND
VÄRMLAND   Västerås   Uppsala
ÖREBRO   UPPLAND
Karlstad   Eskilstuna   STOCKHOLM
Örebro   ★ STOCKHOLM
Mälaren   SÖDERMANLAND
Hjälmaren   Björkö
Tanumshede   Vänern   Nyköping
Lidköping   Norrköping
Uddevalla   Skövde   Linköping
Trollhättan   Vättern   ÖSTERGÖTLAND
VÄSTRA
Göteborg   GÖTALAND   Jönköping   Visby   Fårö
Borås   JÖNKÖPING   GOTLAND
GÖTALAND   Gotland
HALLAND   KALMAR
Halmstad   Växjö   Kalmar
KRONOBERG   Öland
Ängelholm   BLEKINGE
Helsingborg   Kristianstad   Karlskrona
Landskrona   SKÅNE
Malmö   Lund

CHAPTER 2

History

Fourteen thousand years ago, the whole of the country we now know as Sweden was covered by thick ice. Gradually the ice began to melt and, as it retreated northwards, humans followed on to the newly revealed land. The earliest known human habitation in Sweden, in the south of the country, dates from around 12,000 BC. The first settlers were hunters and fishers who made stone tools. After about 1,800 BC, bronze weapons and other objects became widespread, and after about 500 BC iron working began in the region. Settled communities became established as people started to farm the land.

THE SUIONES

The early Swedes were intrepid sailors, and as early as 1,500 BC had extensive trade routes as far south as the River Danube. Archaeological finds in Sweden have shown that trade with the Roman Empire, far to the south, later became well established. In AD 98 the Roman historian, Tacitus, described the Swedes as a tribe of people called the Suiones, who lived on an 'island' in the Baltic and had powerful fleets of ships with prows at both ends, 'so that the boat can advance head-on in either direction'.

THE SWEDISH VIKINGS

From about AD 800, people from southern Scandinavia (present-day Sweden, Denmark and Norway) started to raid and conquer lands overseas. These people spoke a language called Norse and they became known as Vikings,

▼ These Bronze Age rock carvings at Tanumshede on the west coast of Sweden show ships and battles, as well as hunting and fishing scenes.

from the Norse word 'vik' for 'bay' or 'inlet'. It is thought that the Viking expansion was partly a result of overpopulation at home. The Swedish Vikings headed east across the Baltic Sea and along rivers that took them deep into Russia, where they traded for warm furs and amber. They crossed the Black Sea to reach Constantinople (today's Istanbul), the capital of the Byzantine Empire, from where they brought back gold and silver, and luxury cloth.

? Did you know?

The Latin word 'Suiones' is similar to the Anglo-Saxon 'Sweon', from which the English word 'Sweden' is derived. The Swedes' own name for their country is Sverige, meaning 'Land of the Svears', referring to a group of people who first settled in the region around Lake Mälaren but gradually came to dominate most of the country.

Focus on: A Viking town

The town of Birka lies on the island of Björkö, west of present-day Stockholm. It was founded in the late eighth century and abandoned about 200 years later, although it is not clear why. Excavations of this Viking town have revealed that it was well protected, with defensive ramparts and a fortress to house its people if the town was attacked. It is thought that between 500 and 1,000 people lived in Birka, and about 1,600 burial sites have been discovered on the site. According to Norse beliefs, people were buried with objects that could be useful in the life after death. In these graves, archaeologists have found weapons, food and drink, clothes – including fine furs and oriental silks – Arabic coins, pottery and glass. All these finds point to the immense wealth of this trading town.

► These grave markers on Öland Island off the east coast of Sweden date from the Iron Age. The windmill in the distance is one of about 400 that stand on the island.

THE ARRIVAL OF CHRISTIANITY

Christianity arrived in Sweden in 829 with the missionary Ansgar, who came from Germany. However, it was not until the eleventh century that the Christian faith began to take over from the traditional beliefs of the Norse religion. Around the same time, Denmark, Norway and Sweden began to emerge as separate kingdoms while, by 1249, most of Finland was under the control of Sweden, after campaigns led by successive Swedish kings.

THE HANSEATIC LEAGUE

The thirteenth and fourteenth centuries saw the rise in importance of the Hanseatic League (Hansa) in Sweden. This was a powerful alliance of German trading cities under the leadership of the city of Lübeck. Hanseatic traders established an important base at Visby on Gotland; other trading towns including Stockholm also developed during this period.

The German merchants dominated trade in the Baltic area, and German influence was felt throughout the region in architecture, fashions and even in the Swedish language which absorbed many German words.

THE KALMAR UNION

In 1350 disaster came to Sweden in the form of the bubonic plague, known as the Black Death, which killed one-third of the population of the country. Many farms were abandoned as there were not enough people to work on the land. This crisis, coupled with concerns about the power of the Hansa, led to the Kalmar Union in 1397 in which Sweden, Norway and Denmark

▼ Women wear traditional clothes during a medieval re-enactment in Visby on Gotland Island, off Sweden's east coast.

were united under the same monarch. The Kalmar Union lasted for over a century but it was marked by conflict in Sweden between those who supported it and those who opposed it. In 1520, 80 leading Swedish noblemen were executed in Stockholm – the so-called 'Stockholm bloodbath' – on the orders of the Danish union king, Kristian II. This act prompted a revolt led by the Swedish nobleman Gustav Eriksson Vasa, which brought the Kalmar Union to an end in 1521. Two years later, Gustav was crowned king of Sweden.

THE VASAS

Gustav I Vasa (reigned 1523-60) proved to be a powerful and effective monarch, laying the foundations of the modern Swedish state. He confiscated the property and land of the Roman Catholic Church and supported the introduction of the Reformation into Sweden, making the Lutheran Church the national state religion. He also strengthened the power of the monarchy. Swedish kings had always been elected, but this process led to power struggles between the nobles. In 1544 Gustav made the monarchy hereditary – meaning that on his death the Crown would automatically pass to his eldest son. This resulted in the Vasa dynasty continuing for more than a hundred years, despite challenges from the nobles.

Did you know?

The first Swedish king to accept the Christian faith was King Olof Skötkonung, who was baptized in 1008.

▼ Kalmar Slott (Kalmar Castle) stands guarded by walls and bastions on a small island along the Slottsfjarden on Sweden's east coast. The Kalmar Union was proclaimed in this castle.

EMPIRE BUILDING

Under the rule of the Vasas, Sweden expanded its territories through a series of wars. Gustav II Adolf (reigned 1611-32) was a particularly brilliant military leader who won battles against Denmark, Poland and Russia. He involved Sweden in the Thirty Years' War (1618-48), a religious conflict between Catholics and Protestants that affected most of Europe. Gustav II Adolf was killed on the battlefield at Lützen. By the middle of the seventeenth century, Sweden was a powerful force in northern Europe, controlling a large empire that extended across much of Scandinavia and into Russia. It even briefly had a small colony in North America on the Delaware River. But Sweden's economy was still based on agriculture, and it lacked the resources to maintain its position. During the Napoleonic Wars at the beginning of the nineteenth century, Sweden lost much of its empire. It did, however, gain Norway, which was united with Sweden from 1814 until 1905.

MASS EMIGRATION

The short war fought with Norway in 1814 was the last time Sweden became directly involved in a war, as the country adopted a policy of neutrality (see page 34). Peace and stability during the nineteenth century led to a massive increase in Sweden's population, from 1.8 million in 1750 to 3.5 million in 1850. However, lack of jobs, failed harvests and famine forced many Swedes to leave their country. Between 1851 and 1930, nearly 1.5 million Swedes emigrated, most to start new lives in North America. The resulting fall in population led directly to the establishment of national policies to help women combine work and family life (see page 33) to try to promote population growth.

Focus on: Queen Kristina

When Gustav II Adolf died in 1632, his six-year-old daughter, Kristina, succeeded to the throne. Until she came of age, her father's chancellor, Axel Oxenstierna, ruled Sweden and continued Gustav's exploits abroad. When she was old enough, Queen Kristina ruled over a glittering court which attracted artists and scholars from all over Europe. Despite her Protestant upbringing, Kristina was attracted to the Roman Catholic faith and in 1654 she abdicated and left for Rome, where she converted to Catholicism. She was the last monarch of the Vasa dynasty.

◀ Gustav II Adolf was one of Sweden's greatest kings, sometimes referred to as the 'Lion of the North'.

INDUSTRIALIZATION

The late nineteenth and early twentieth centuries saw the rapid industrialization of the Swedish economy. Trade unions were established and the right to vote was given to men in 1909 and to women in 1921. During the two world wars that tore Europe apart during the twentieth century, Sweden held fast to its policy of neutrality. The welfare state, set up after the Second World War, helped to provide financial security and essential services for all Swedes, with provisions such as unemployment payments and free childcare. Throughout the 1950s and 1960s, living standards improved dramatically, fuelled by Sweden's booming economy.

▼ Mourners gather in the streets of Stockholm for the funeral of the Swedish premier, Olof Palme, in 1986.

AN OPEN SOCIETY

In 1986, people in Sweden and across the world were stunned to learn of the assassination of the Swedish prime minister, Olof Palme, on the streets of Stockholm. No one knows who committed the murder but, in the aftermath, many Swedes stressed the continuing importance of the egalitarian and non-violent values that lie at the heart of their society and culture. These values were once again emphasized following the equally shocking murder, also in Stockholm, of Foreign Minister Anna Lindh in 2003. Ironically, in both cases one of the reasons the killers had been able to target their victims was because of the lack of heavy security for leading politicians. Protection for prominent public figures in Sweden has been tightened up since Anna Lindh's murder.

CHAPTER 3

Landscape and Climate

Sweden covers a total area of 449,964 sq km (173,731 sq miles). It is a long, thin country, with a maximum distance of 1,574 km (977 miles) from north to south and 499 km (310 miles) from east to west. It has a long, rugged coastline stretching from the Gulf of Bothnia in the north, south to the Baltic Sea and west to the Kattegat, the channel that lies between Sweden and Denmark. There are many islands off Sweden's coast, the largest of which, Gotland and Öland, lie in the Baltic Sea. Sweden's mainland has a variety of landscapes, from the rugged mountains of the north-west to the fertile plains of the south-east. There are thousands of lakes across the country, the largest of which are Vänern (5,584 sq km/ 2,156 sq miles) and Vättern (1,911 sq km/ 738 sq miles).

NORRLAND

Sweden's terrain can be divided into three main regions: Norrland, Svealand and Götaland.

▼ A river valley in Sarek National Park in Norrland. The park is an area of mountain wilderness that covers 197,000 hectares.

Norrland covers the northern three-fifths of the country. In the west of this region, the Kölen Mountains form the border between Sweden and Norway. Sweden's highest point, Kebnekaise (Mount Kebne) is among these mountains and reaches 2,111 m (6,926 ft). Sweden's largest rivers originate in the Kölen Mountains and flow south-east across the Northern Highlands to the Gulf of Bothnia. The Northern Highlands is a sparsely populated area of forest, rivers and lakes, with fertile valleys opening out towards the coast.

The far north of Norrland lies well within the Arctic Circle, so people in this region experience long summer days and long winter nights. In fact, during the month of June there is 24-hour daylight as the sun never dips below the horizon. But in midwinter, from mid-December to mid-January, there is 24-hour darkness as the sun does not appear above the horizon. During these days of darkness, the Aurora Borealis (Northern Lights) can often be seen illuminating the sky with spectacular and colourful effects.

SVEALAND AND GÖTALAND

South of Norrland lies Svealand, 'Land of the Svears' (see page 9). This region is the most densely populated in Sweden and consists of farmland interspersed with hills, woodland and lakes. It includes the Swedish capital, Stockholm. The southernmost region of Sweden, Götaland, is made up of dense forests and farmland and includes lakes Vänern and Vättern. Skåne, in the far south, has the richest agricultural land in the country.

▶ A farm on the edge of Lake Vättern. The lake, the second largest in Sweden (after Vänern), is noted for the cleanliness of its water.

> ### Focus on: A landscape shaped by ice
>
> Sweden's landscape has been shaped by the ice that covered the country thousands of years ago. The weight and movement of these great ice sheets created smooth-sided valleys and deep lakes, and sculpted the distinctive shapes of the Kölen Mountains. Fast-moving glacial rivers deposited sand and silt to form the fertile soils of the central plains. Today, small glaciers remain on many of the mountains in the far north.

SWEDEN'S CLIMATE

Sweden enjoys a warmer climate than its northern location might suggest. This is because of the warming effect of the Gulf Stream, an ocean current that flows in the Atlantic northwards from the Equator and brings mild, wet weather to Sweden's south-western coast. Generally, the weather in Sweden can be quite changeable, with sunshine and rain following in quick succession.

Sweden's long length means that its climate differs from north to south. This difference is most marked in the winter, when the north can be blanketed in thick snow while the south experiences rainfall. The average minimum temperature for January in Göteborg on

Sweden's west coast is -3°C (26.6°F), while in Piteå in the north of the Gulf of Bothnia it is -13°C (8.6°F), and has been known to drop to -38°C (-36.4°F). Snow starts to fall in the north as early as September and stays on the ground until April or May, when spring finally arrives. The waters of the Gulf of Bothnia freeze every

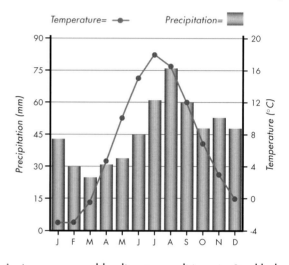

▲ Average monthly climate conditions in Stockholm

▼ A winter landscape in Södermanland in eastern Sweden. Winters can be long and very cold in parts of Sweden.

winter. In central Sweden, the snows come later and melt sooner, while the south of Sweden is often snow-free all winter. The waters around southern Sweden very seldom freeze.

SUMMERTIME

The Swedish summer lasts from mid June to mid August. Differences between the north and the south are far less marked during these months thanks to the long days in the north, which raise temperatures. As a result, in both Piteå and Göteborg, the average maximum temperature in July is 21°C (69.8°F).

? Did you know?

The temperature is below freezing point for an average of 71 days in the year in Malmö, southern Sweden. At Haparanda, near the Arctic Circle in northern Sweden, the temperature remains below freezing for an average of 184 days per year.

Focus on: Sweden's forests

More than half of Sweden's land area is covered with trees – deciduous forests in the south and coniferous forests in the north. Deciduous trees such as beech, oak, elm, ash and lime grow in the southernmost regions, and in the springtime the floors of these forests are covered in a profusion of wild flowers. Further north, spruce and pine are the main coniferous trees. In the mountainous regions, the hardy birch, a deciduous tree, grows at higher altitudes than the coniferous forest. Beneath the birch trees, woody shrubs such as crowberry, bilberry and whortleberry flourish, and picking these berries and finding edible fungi are popular weekend pastimes for Swedes in late summer and early autumn.

▼ A man and his young son gather wild mushrooms while checking a mushroom guide in a forest close to Skokloster in the Uppland area.

CHAPTER 4

Population and Settlements

Sweden has a population of 9 million people. Up until the middle of the twentieth century, this population was almost entirely made up of native-born Swedes, with small Finnish and Sami (see box opposite) minorities. But since the Second World War there has been steady immigration into Sweden from countries all over the world. The arrival of immigrants has raised many issues about how these 'new Swedes' should be integrated into Swedish society.

IMMIGRATION AND EMIGRATION

Although Sweden has a long history of people settling within its borders – for example, the German Hansa merchants of the thirteenth and fourteenth centuries (see page 10) – until the twentieth century immigration was not sufficiently large scale to have any significant effect on the population structure. The waves of emigration in the late nineteenth and early twentieth centuries (see page 12), however, did have an effect. The loss of 1.5 million people from a population of between 4 and 5 million led to labour shortages when the Swedish economy began to expand in the 1950s. Refugees from surrounding countries made up the first wave of immigrants during the Second World War. They were followed in the 1950s and 1960s by people from countries such as Finland, the former Yugoslavia, Greece, Italy, Turkey and Poland, most of whom came to Sweden to find work.

▼ People on a street in Göteborg, on the west coast of Sweden. Göteborg has a large number of immigrant residents amounting to roughly 20 per cent of the city's population.

During the 1970s, the demand for labour in Sweden decreased. The Swedish government placed restrictions on immigration and the number of people coming to Sweden fell.

However, since the 1980s, Sweden has been generous in its provision of sanctuary for large numbers of refugees and asylum-seekers, including Kurds from Turkey and Iran, and people from Iraq, Chile and the former Yugoslavia. Today, foreign-born or first-generation immigrants make up about 10 per cent of the Swedish population.

Population data

- Population: 9 million
- Population 0-14 yrs: 17%
- Population 15-64 yrs: 65%
- Population 65+ yrs: 18%
- Population growth rate: 0.3%
- Population density: 20 per sq km/51.8 per sq mile
- Urban population: 83%
- Major cities:
  Stockholm 1,729,000
  Göteborg   829,000

Source: United Nations and World Bank

Focus on: Sami life

The Sami live in a region known as Sápmi (Lappland) that extends across northern Sweden, Norway, Finland and Russia. It is estimated that there are between 70,000 and 80,000 Sami, and that between 17,000 and 20,000 live in Sweden. Traditional Sami occupations were reindeer herding, hunting, fishing and farming. Today only a small number of Sami continue to herd reindeer, but the animal remains very important in Sami culture. Many Sami work in tourism, mining, fishing or farming. They have their own language and musical and artistic traditions, many of which can be experienced at the famous market and festival which is held in Jokkmokk, northern Sweden, every February.

▼ Sami in a traditional *kata* (hut) in Arvidsjaur, Norrland, where a complete Sami village has been preserved.

A MULTICULTURAL SOCIETY?

When immigrants first began to arrive in Sweden, it was presumed that these people would adopt the language and customs of their new country and become 'Swedes'. Then, in the 1970s, the Swedish government revised these ideas and set out new guidelines under three headings: equality, freedom of cultural choice, and co-operation and solidarity. The aim was to give immigrants equal rights with the rest of the Swedish population, to allow them to choose how far they wished to adopt Swedish customs, and to work together to resolve problems and issues.

Since the 1980s, however, Sweden has struggled to cope with the number of people seeking refuge within its borders. Problems with the economy have led to high unemployment, resulting in many immigrants being unable to get jobs and relying on Sweden's welfare system to survive. Tensions between different communities have resulted in racist attacks, such as the ones that occurred in 1993 in Trollhättan, near Göteborg in western Sweden, when two Somali immigrants were badly beaten and the local mosque was burned down. In reaction to those attacks, the municipal council in Trollhättan has worked hard to resolve its problems through improved education, better facilities for its immigrant population and a zero-tolerance approach to racism.

WHERE DO PEOPLE LIVE?

Sweden has a very low population density and large areas of the country are uninhabited. The average population density for the whole country is 20 people per sq km (51.8 per sq mile), but there is a wide range from 253 people per sq km in Stockholm to only 3 people per sq km in Norrbotten, the most northerly of the Swedish counties. Eighty-three per cent of Sweden's population are urban dwellers, with only 17 per cent living in the countryside. Most of the population is centred in the south, particularly around the large conurbations of Stockholm, Göteborg and Malmö. Many

▼ A Turkish woman at work in the kitchen of a restaurant in Rinkeby, a suburb of Stockholm with a very high immigrant population.

immigrants and their children have found themselves living on the outskirts of Sweden's major cities, often in communities with other immigrants, leading to fears about racial segregation and discrimination.

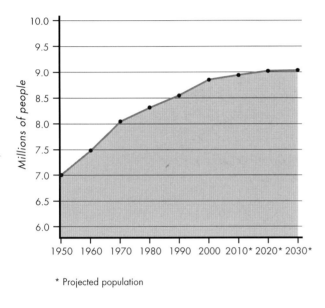

* Projected population

▲ Population growth, 1950-2030

Focus on: Stockholm

The Swedish capital, Stockholm, lies on the country's eastern coast. Known as the 'city that floats on water', the central part of this beautiful city is built on 14 islands where Lake Mälaren meets the Saltsjön (Salt Sea) on the Baltic coast. The population of Stockholm municipality is 765,000, while the greater urban area that forms the conurbation of Stockholm has a population of 1,729,000, making it the largest city in Scandinavia. A large number of foreign citizens, including Finns, Iranians, Iraqis, Chileans and Turks, are permanent residents of Stockholm. There are many local schemes to help these immigrant populations feel at home in Swedish society. For example, the Livstycket Association, which is based in a district of Stockholm with a large immigrant population, encourages people to create textile art and clothing while at the same time helping them to learn the Swedish language.

► A timber house in the Swedish countryside. Many houses in Sweden are made from wood, as it is a plentiful resource. They are often also painted in this colour, called Falun red (see page 30).

CHAPTER 5

Government and Politics

Sweden is a democratic country, with an elected parliament and a hereditary monarchy. The present king, Carl XVI Gustaf, came to the throne in 1973. He is a descendant of one of Napoleon Bonaparte's marshals, Jean Baptiste Bernadotte, who was elected to be the Swedish king in 1810, and was crowned in 1818 as King Karl XIV Johan. The heir to the throne is the king's eldest daughter, Crown Princess Victoria, in line with a new Act of Succession adopted in 1980 which gave the right of succession to the eldest child of the monarch, whether male or female. Before this, male children held precedence over female children.

▼ The Swedish Riksdagshuset (parliament building) in Stockholm. The building lies on a small island called Helgeandsholmen in the city.

THE SWEDISH PARLIAMENT

'All public power in Sweden comes from the people.' This is the first sentence of the Swedish constitution and it reflects the importance to the Swedish people of their democratic and egalitarian society. The Swedish parliament is the Riksdag, and it has 349 members. These members of parliament (MPs) are elected every four years in general elections. Every Swedish citizen aged 18 or over has the right to vote, and participation in general elections is usually high – in the 2002 election it was 80.1 per cent of the voting population.

The Riksdag appoints a prime minister who then chooses ministers to lead the various departments covering areas such as defence, agriculture, foreign affairs, health, justice and

sustainable development. Together, the prime minister (who since 1996 has been the Social Democrat, Göran Persson) and his or her ministers form the government of Sweden.

POLITICAL PARTIES

Today, seven political parties are represented in the Riksdag: the Social Democrats, the Moderates, the Liberals, the Christian Democrats, the Centre Party, the Left Party and the Green Party. The Social Democratic Party is Sweden's largest political party, and it has governed the country almost continuously since the 1930s (except for between 1976 and 1982, and 1991 and 1994). Sweden's political parties can be grouped into socialist (the Social Democrat, Left and Green parties) and non-socialist (Moderate, Liberal, Centre and Christian Democrat parties), but Swedish politics operates largely on the principle of consensus, with different parties often working together to achieve a common aim.

Focus on: Neo-Nazis

In 1999, the murder of a trade union activist called Björn Söderberg was just one of several fatal incidents involving neo-Nazi groups that sparked off nationwide rallies to protest about the increasing violence. According to a Swedish government report published in 2001, the growth of extreme racist groups in Sweden and abroad, known as the 'white power' movement, has been helped by the ease of communication and anonymity offered by the Internet.

? *Did you know?*

Women are well represented in the Swedish parliament, with the proportion of women MPs standing at 45.3 per cent after the 2002 election.

▼ Inside the Riksdagshuset, members of parliament sit in the main chamber.

LOCAL GOVERNMENT

Sweden is divided into 21 regions, or counties, and 290 municipalities. Elections for county and municipal councils occur every four years at the same time as the general elections. Foreign nationals who have lived in Sweden for three years or more may vote in county and municipal elections, although they are not permitted to vote in a general election. County councils are responsible for healthcare in their regions; they also promote regional growth, for example, by supporting local businesses. The municipal councils provide education, childcare and care for the elderly, and are responsible for a wide range of services including housing, emergency services, water supplies and waste management, energy supply, and cultural and recreational facilities. These services are funded through local income taxes which are set by the municipal and county councils and which, on average, are about 30 per cent of taxable income. In recent years, many municipal councils have also taken responsibility for increasing numbers of refugee inhabitants, for which they are given special funds directly from the national government.

SWEDEN AND THE EUROPEAN UNION

Sweden became a member of the European Union (EU) in 1995, after a referendum (national vote) which showed that many Swedes were uncertain about becoming more closely linked with their European neighbours – 52.3 per cent of Swedes voted to join, but 46.8 per cent voted against. In 1999, the EU introduced a common currency, the Euro, in 11

▼ 'Vote no' ('Rösta nej') reads this banner in the run-up to the referendum in 1994 on whether Sweden should become a member of the European Union.

of its then 15 member countries. Sweden was one of the countries that decided not to take part, and in 2003 this decision was finalized by another referendum in which 55.9 per cent of Swedes rejected the Euro. Differences of opinion about the EU have had an effect on national politics, with the Left Party leading the 'No' campaign against the Euro while the Social Democrats were divided over the issue, although the party officially supported the 'Yes' campaign.

TAXES AND THE WELFARE STATE

Sweden is renowned for its welfare provision, paid for by the highest taxes of any country in the world. On average, people pay a local tax of between 29 and 34 per cent and a further national tax of 20 per cent for higher earners (compared with 22 per cent basic rate, and a higher rate of 40 per cent in the UK). The aim has been to redistribute income so that all members of society have equal access to education, healthcare, childcare and other services. However, since the 1980s Sweden has struggled to cope with the increased demands on its welfare state, and funding has decreased as a result of the economic crisis of the early 1990s (see page 30). Nevertheless, the welfare state remains an important part of Swedish society and one that many Swedes prize very highly.

? Did you know?

A high proportion of Sweden's GDP is made up of tax revenues. In 2003, the figure was 50.7 per cent compared with 35.6 per cent in the UK and 25.6 per cent in the USA.

Focus on: The Sami Parliament

In 1993, King Carl XVI Gustaf opened the first Sami Parliament in Kiruna, northern Sweden. The parliament decides how to distribute money from the Swedish government to Sami organizations, and deals with matters such as land use, fishing and hunting, which are of great importance to the Sami people. It is also involved in the management of Sami schools (see page 43).

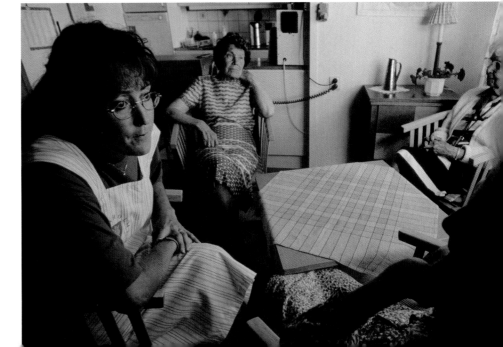

▶ A member of the care staff talks to three residents of a state-run home for the elderly in Stockholm. State-funded care for children and for older people is given a high priority in Sweden.

CHAPTER 6

Energy and Resources

Sweden has no oil or coal reserves, and it imports all of the oil it needs for energy production and other uses. However, the country does have huge potential for renewable energy, including water and wind power and the burning of biofuels (see page 28), and these are playing an increasingly important part in the country's energy policy. Sweden has large mineral reserves, including iron ore, copper and silver, and these form the basis for a large sector of the country's economy.

HEP

Sweden has been making use of its many rivers to produce electricity since the 1880s, and the use of hydro-electric power (HEP) has expanded rapidly since the 1930s. However, in the 1960s, concern about the environmental effects of constructing dams led to a government decision not to build any hydro-power facilities on the four major undammed rivers in northern Sweden, although hydro-electric plants continued to be used and developed elsewhere. Today, hydro-electric power continues to play an important part in Sweden's energy mix, making up 45.6 per cent of electricity production.

NUCLEAR POWER

Before the 1970s, Sweden relied almost entirely on HEP and imported oil for its energy requirements. But the oil crisis in the 1970s, when oil prices rose rapidly and supplies from the Middle East were cut off to many countries, led the Swedish government to turn to nuclear power for electricity generation.

▼ Felled tree trunks are stacked on to a trailer in Sundsvall. In Sweden, biofuels produced from the wastes from timber processing are an increasingly important energy resource.

Six nuclear power stations were opened in the 1970s, and another six in the 1980s. But, after a referendum held in 1980, the Swedish government decided to close down its nuclear power stations by 2010 if alternative energy sources could be found and relied upon. The Chernobyl disaster in 1986, which badly affected Sweden (see box below), reinforced public concern about the safety of nuclear power. However, the biggest advantage of nuclear power is that it does not add to carbon dioxide (CO_2) emissions, the so-called 'greenhouse gases'. Today, 46.3 per cent of Sweden's electricity is still produced by nuclear power and, because there is a high priority given in Sweden to the reduction of CO_2 emissions, public opinion is largely in favour of continuing to use the existing reactors until the end of their natural lives. Nevertheless, the government is still planning to phase out nuclear power.

Focus on: Chernobyl

In April 1986, a huge explosion at a nuclear power plant in the Soviet Union sent radioactive material into the atmosphere across much of northern Europe. The north of Sweden was badly hit by the fallout, particularly as large amounts of radioactive material were distributed by heavy rains that fell in the days following the Chernobyl explosion. Since 1986, studies of the affected areas have linked a rise in the number of people suffering from various forms of cancer with the increase in radiation.

Energy data

▻ Energy consumption as % of world total: 0.5%

▻ Energy consumption by sector (% of total),

Industry:	35.9
Transportation:	23.0
Agriculture:	1.4
Services:	13.7
Residential:	22.6
Other:	3.4

▻ CO_2 emissions as % of world total: 0.2

▻ CO_2 emissions per capita in tonnes p.a.: 5.5

Source: World Resources Institute

▼ Barsebäck nuclear power station in southern Sweden was built in the 1960s and fully closed down in 2005.

▲ A wind turbine near the village of Simrishamn in the region of Skåne. In the future, increasing amounts of energy will be produced by wind power in Sweden.

RENEWABLE ENERGY

In an effort to replace nuclear power, the Swedish government is investing heavily in renewable forms of energy. Sweden is one of the world leaders in the use of biofuels as an energy source. Biofuels are fuels that are produced from organic matter, in Sweden mostly wastes from timber processing, such as wood chips and sawdust. This waste is burned to produce electricity and generate heat. In some Swedish cities, biofuels provide the heat for district heating systems – where hot water is pumped through pipes to provide heating and hot water supplies for all the homes and businesses in a particular area. In the southern city of Lund, the district heating system is supplied by geothermal energy. Hot water is pumped from deep below the earth's surface (about 3,500 m/11,483 ft) and, once the heat energy has been used, is then pumped back into the ground. This project has significantly reduced the use of oil in the city, and therefore has also reduced CO_2 emissions.

Wind power is another potential energy source that the Swedish government plans to exploit further in the future. There are plans for new wind farms along the coast and around Lake Vänern, and for an offshore wind farm in the Öresund sea strait between southern Sweden and Denmark.

NATURAL RESOURCES

Sweden is the largest producer of iron ore in the European Union, and a major iron ore exporter. It is also a leading producer of other metals, such as copper, lead, zinc, silver and gold. The mining industry is based in the north of the country, and exploration for new reserves is ongoing, with new mines continuing to open. Sweden has made use of its abundant mineral resources to become a major producer of high-quality iron and steel. The Swedish steel industry is highly modernized: computers are used to make every process as efficient as possible, and the impact on the environment is given a high priority, which means that energy consumption and emissions are low compared with similar industries in other countries.

Timber is another major resource in Sweden. Forests cover up to three quarters of the country, and timber and related products make up about 12 per cent of Sweden's export income. Timber is used for building, and for the manufacture of furniture and other items. The by-products of these timber industries provide an important source of biofuels.

Sweden's long coastline and easy access to the sea mean that fish has always played an important part in the national diet (see page 47). Today the fishing industry employs around 4,000 people in Sweden, about half of whom work on boats catching fish, another 1,800 in the fish processing industry, and another 300 in aquaculture (fish farming). The bulk of the catch is made up of cod, herring, sprat and prawns. Sweden's inland waters, particularly the large southern lakes of Vänern, Hjälmaren,

Mälaren and Vättern, are also an important source of fish such as pike, perch and vendace. However, although fishing plays an important role in the local economy in many places, it is a relatively small industry in Sweden, accounting for just 0.2 per cent of GDP.

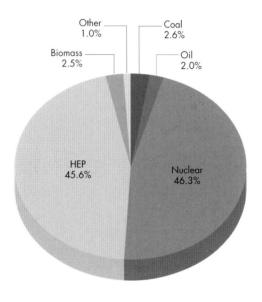

▲ Electricity production by type

▼ A fishing boat is surrounded by seagulls off Västra Götaland, on the west coast. There are many fishing villages along this rugged coastline.

CHAPTER 7

Economy and Income

During the twentieth century, Sweden rapidly transformed itself from an agricultural country to an industrial one. It based its industrialization on its natural resources – iron ore, timber and plentiful HEP to provide energy. However, because of the relatively small home market, Swedish companies have always looked abroad to sell their products. This early emphasis on export and globalization has resulted in the development of a large number of multinational companies which have their roots in Sweden, including household names such as Volvo, Saab, Ikea, Ericsson, H&M and Electrolux.

ECONOMIC CRISIS AND RECOVERY

The development of Sweden's industries throughout much of the twentieth century resulted in steady economic growth. However, in the early 1990s this growth was interrupted as the country entered a period of economic crisis. An international recession led to a reduction in demand for Swedish products and a corresponding drop in manufacturing output. Unemployment rose rapidly to 8 per cent from an average of 2 or 3 per cent throughout the 1980s. Low levels of manufacturing output and high levels of unemployment, coupled with a population growth partly resulting from immigration (see page 19) and the demands of the welfare state (see page 25) left the Swedish government struggling to cope. In 1993,

? Did you know?

Agriculture accounts for only 2 per cent of the labour force in Sweden, and only 7 per cent of the land is suitable for farming.

▼ An iron smelter in Falun, Dalarna, a mining area in central Sweden. Falun is famous for its red paint, traditionally produced from the waste products of the local copper mines.

Sweden's budget deficit (the amount by which a government's spending exceeds its income) rose to 12 per cent of GDP, the highest figure for any industrialized nation that year.

Cutbacks on spending on the welfare state and increased demand for exports saw the Swedish economy begin to recover in 1994, and industrial production increased throughout the remainder of the 1990s. However, there was a shift in emphasis away from traditional industries, such as steel and timber, towards more high-tech sectors, such as telecommunications and IT, in which many Swedish companies are world leaders. By 1998, the budget deficit had turned into a budget surplus and, by 2000, levels of unemployment had dropped to around 4 per cent.

Economic data

- Gross National Income (GNI) in US$: 321,401,159,680
- World rank by GNI: 19
- GNI per capita in US$: 35,770
- World rank by GNI per capita: 10
- Economic growth: 3.6%

Source: World Bank

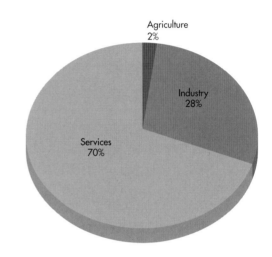

▲ Contribution by sector to national income

Focus on: Tetra Pak

In 1950, the Swedish entrepreneur, Dr Ruben Rausing, founded the first packaging company. In 1952, his company launched its first product – Tetra Classic – a tetrahedron-shaped (four-sided) carton made from plastic-coated cardboard which was used for storing and transporting milk and cream. Rausing had been working on the development of this revolutionary packaging since 1943. Today, Tetra Pak is a multinational company with more than 20,000 employees worldwide, although the business is still owned by the Rausing family. Tetra Pak continues to innovate, with products such as Tetra Recart, which allows foods that are traditionally packaged in metal cans and glass jars to be packaged in square-shaped cartons. Tetra Recart was launched in the USA in 2004.

▲ A worker in a Volvo truck factory in Göteborg. Volvo is an important employer in the city.

RESEARCH AND DEVELOPMENT

Sweden has become known as a world leader for innovation, research and design. Spending on research and development is particularly high in companies specializing in telecommunications, pharmaceuticals and transport equipment. The importance of these sectors is reflected in the export statistics, where chemical products (which include pharmaceuticals) make up 12.1 per cent of the total value, electric and electronic equipment make up 15.5 per cent and transport equipment makes up 15.2 per cent. Although a high proportion of research work is carried out by the multinational companies that are based in Sweden, the Swedish government has for many years emphasized the importance of development and innovation by funding research departments in Sweden's universities. It has also set up several councils which undertake research in various fields, including social sciences, medicine, engineering sciences and education.

▼ A container and bulk cargo terminal for shipping in Stockholm.

WORKING IN SWEDEN

A large proportion of the Swedish workforce is employed by the public sector, for example, in schools, hospitals, childcare and caring for the elderly. The number of people employed by national government, municipal and county councils amounted to 41 per cent of the workforce in 1990, although after cutbacks during the economic crisis this figure had fallen to 34 per cent by 2001. However, many services that were under government control have been opened up to competition by the Swedish government, notably the post service, railways and the electricity supply. This lessening of state control has helped to boost growth and create more jobs in the private sector.

Relations between managers and employees have traditionally been good in Sweden. A large number of employees are members of trade unions, which are a powerful force in the country. Decisions about pay increases and working conditions are made through nationwide negotiation (known as collective bargaining) between union representatives and employers, rather than being imposed by the

government. The structure of companies also tends to be less hierarchical than in many other countries, with smaller differences in pay between managers and their employees, and an emphasis on teamwork and agreement within a company. However, there is concern about the number of highly qualified young Swedes who choose to go abroad to work in countries such as the USA, where they can earn more than they do in Sweden.

? Did you know?

About 47 per cent of the Swedish population belongs to the workforce.

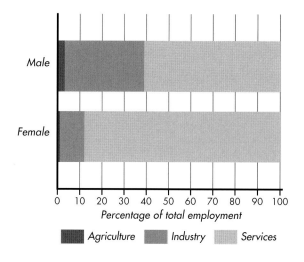

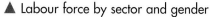

Percentage of total employment

■ Agriculture ■ Industry ▨ Services

▲ Labour force by sector and gender

Focus on: Women and childcare

Since the 1960s, the Swedish government has put policies in place to encourage women to work. In particular, Sweden has an extensive network of nurseries and pre-schools, which allows parents to work full-time if they wish to. The cost of childcare is largely met by revenue from taxes (see page 25), but parents also pay a fee which is based on their income. Parents are entitled to a generous amount of parental leave when a child is born – 480 days' leave can be taken by either parent.

◀ Children sit at a table with a carer to eat cereal at a nursery in Stockholm. This daycare centre is funded and run by the state.

CHAPTER 8

Global Connections

Since the beginning of its history, Sweden has been a trading nation, with links across Europe. Today these links are worldwide, as Sweden exports a large proportion of the goods and services made within its borders. Sweden also plays an important role in international organizations such as the United Nations (UN) and the European Union, which it joined in 1995 (see page 24).

SWEDEN AND NEUTRALITY

Since the early nineteenth century, Sweden has had a policy of neutrality in armed conflicts. The policy was adopted after the Napoleonic Wars (see page 12), during which Sweden lost much of its empire. In the twentieth century Sweden held fast to its neutrality throughout the First and Second World Wars. However, Sweden could not remain untouched by events

in Europe during these wars. When the Soviet Union attacked Finland in 1939, thousands of Swedes went to help the Finns in the fight against the Red (Soviet) Army. Later, after Germany had invaded and occupied Denmark and Norway, Sweden allowed unarmed German troops to travel through its territories to and from Norway. And Sweden's policy of neutrality did not prevent it from building up its own armed forces so that it could defend itself in case of attack. Today, the defence industry is an important sector in Sweden's economy, with companies such as BAE Systems, Saab and Ericsson involved in the manufacture and export of armaments and defence systems.

▼ Cranes are used to load ships at the docks in Göteborg. The city has long been a centre of trade and commerce, and the port is the largest in Scandinavia.

NATO INVOLVEMENT

After the end of the Second World War, Norway and Denmark became members of the North Atlantic Treaty Organization (NATO), set up in 1949 to 'promote stability and well-being in the North Atlantic area'. Sweden remained outside NATO, preferring to continue with its policy of 'non-participation in alliances in time of peace, aiming at neutrality in the event of war'. However, in the 1990s Sweden became a member of NATO's Partnership for Peace (PfP) and Europe-Atlantic Partnership Council (EAPC). The PfP was set up in 1994 after the break-up of the Soviet Union and the end of the Cold War. An aim of the PfP is to promote co-operation between countries over security and defence. The EAPC, set up in 1997, offers an opportunity for regular meetings between representatives from more than 40 countries to discuss matters such as international crisis management and emergency planning.

? Did you know?

Sixty per cent of all goods produced in Sweden are exported.

▶ A Swedish Air Force pilot flies alongside other training jets. The Saab company manufactures vehicles as well as aircraft.

Focus on: Raoul Wallenberg

Raoul Wallenberg (1912-1947) came from one of Sweden's wealthiest and most influential families. He is famous for saving the lives of thousands of Jews during the Second World War. In 1944, Germany invaded the lands of its former ally, Hungary. The Germans immediately began to deport Hungarian Jews to concentration camps in occupied Poland, and Wallenberg went to the Hungarian capital, Budapest, to try to save them. Through a mixture of diplomacy, bribes and threats he managed to set up 'safe houses' in the city where Jews could take refuge. Wallenberg declared the houses to be Swedish territory, which meant that Jews were protected from arrest there. It is estimated that Wallenberg rescued around 100,000 Jews. In 1944, the Soviet army invaded Hungary and Wallenberg disappeared into captivity. The Soviets claim that he died in 1947, but his family does not know exactly what happened to him.

PEACEMAKERS

Sweden has produced some notable peacemakers and negotiators who have played a major role on the world stage. They include Folke Bernadotte, who worked for the United Nations in Palestine before his assassination in 1948, and Dag Hammarskjöld. As Secretary General of the United Nations in 1953, Hammarskjöld used his diplomatic skills to good effect at moments of international tension ranging from the Korean War to the Suez Crisis (1956). In 1961 he died in a plane crash on a UN mission to the Congo in Africa.

Sweden became a member of the UN in 1946. The UN is an important part of Swedish foreign policy, because it is seen as an organization through which smaller countries can play an important role towards world peace. Sweden has sent troops to many trouble spots around the world, including Kosovo and Bosnia, as part of UN peacekeeping operations. It has also provided high-profile negotiators such as Carl Bildt and Hans Blix. Bildt, who was prime minister of Sweden from 1991 to 1994, oversaw the reconstruction of Bosnia-Herzegovina after the civil war in the early 1990s. From 2000 to 2003, Blix headed the UN Monitoring, Verification and Inspection Commission (UNMOVIC), which was in charge of monitoring the disarmament of Iraq's weapons of mass destruction. Blix has criticized both the US and UK governments for the decision to invade Iraq in 2003.

SWEDEN AND THE EU

Since it became a member of the European Union in 1995, Sweden has supported its enlargement. In 2004, the EU welcomed ten new member states into the Union, including the Baltic states of Estonia, Lithuania and Latvia. The Baltic states are of particular importance to Sweden, as they are close neighbours. Swedish banks and companies have invested heavily in the economies of the Baltic states, and their membership of the EU will make trade and regional co-operation easier.

▼ The World Trade Center in Stockholm is a conference and exhibition centre.

Focus on: The Nobel Prize

Alfred Nobel was born in Stockholm in 1833. His father was an engineer, and Alfred followed in his footsteps, studying chemical engineering in Sweden, Germany, France and the USA. After years of dangerous experimentation, in the course of which his brother was killed during an experiment, Nobel developed an explosive material that he called dynamite. This invention revolutionized construction work, such as drilling tunnels and digging canals. Nobel quickly became a very rich man, and founded factories in more than 20 countries worldwide. When he died in 1896, his will stated that his inheritance was to be used for annual prizes to acknowledge great achievement in physics, chemistry, medicine, literature and peace. The awarding of these prestigious prizes continues to this day, with the glittering award ceremony held in the Concert Hall in Stockholm, followed by a banquet in the City Hall.

▲ At the 2002 ceremony in Stockholm, Masatoshi Koshiba (left) won the Nobel Prize for Physics and Koichi Tanaka (right) the Nobel Prize for Chemistry. Winners receive a medal, a personal diploma and prize money.

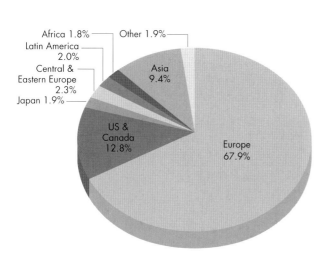

▲ Destination of exports by major trading region

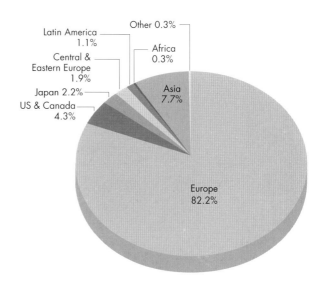

▲ Origin of imports by major trading region

CHAPTER 9

Transport and Communications

S weden is a sparsely populated country, and distances between settlements in the north of the country can be huge. For this reason, good communications and infrastructure have been vital to Sweden's development. Today there is an extensive road system, and even in remote areas roads are well constructed and maintained. There are also extensive ferry, railway and air links.

ROAD AND RAIL

Sweden has 213,237 km (132,505 miles) of roads, and car ownership is high at 452 per 1,000 people. Most families own at least one car. Roads and bridges in Sweden are all toll free, with the exception of the Öresund Link which connects Malmö and the Danish capital, Copenhagen (see box opposite). There are also state-run car ferries, which transport vehicles across short stretches of water in some places.

The rail network reaches from the border with Norway in the north to Sweden's southernmost tip. The state-owned railway company Statens Järnvägar (SJ) operates most of the long distance routes, but private companies such as Connex and Tågkompaniet also operate some train services. A high-speed 'tilting' train known as the X2000 was developed in the 1980s to cope with the curves of many sections of track on Sweden's railways. Other high-speed trains, for example in France and in Japan, run on almost straight, purpose-built track, but Swedish engineers developed tilting technology to allow the trains to run at high speeds around bends. The X2000 was introduced in 1990, and since then it has reduced the rail journey time from Stockholm to Göteborg by an hour. Stockholm is the only Swedish city with an underground railway system.

◀ A bus waits to meet a ferry service from Stockholm that serves the islands and coastal region around the city. Sweden is well known for such integrated transport planning.

The Tunnelbanan, or T-banan, has three lines and about 110 km (68 miles) of track. Göteborg has an extensive and modern tram system linking the centre of the city with its suburbs.

AIR TRAVEL

Stockholm's main international airport is Arlanda, about 40 km (25 miles) north of the city centre. But budget airlines are increasingly using the smaller Skavsta and Västerås airports, which lie about 100 km (62 miles) south and east of the city respectively. Most domestic flights use Bromma airport, which is closest to the city centre. Göteborg and Malmö also have their own airports, and air travel is an important means of getting around Sweden, with a variety of low-cost airlines such as Skyways and Sverigeflyg to choose from.

Transport & communications data

- Total roads: 213,237 km/132,505 miles
- Total paved roads: 167,604 km/ 104,149 miles
- Total unpaved roads: 45,633 km/ 28,356 miles
- Total railways: 11,481 km/7,134 miles
- Airports: 254
- Cars per 1,000 people: 452
- Mobile phones per 1,000 people: 1,034
- Personal computers per 1,000 people: 621.3
- Internet users per 1,000 people: 756

Source: World Bank and CIA World Factbook

Focus on: The Öresund Link

The Danish capital, Copenhagen, and the Swedish city of Malmö are separated by a 14-km (9-mile) channel called the Öresund. The idea of building a link between the two has been debated since the nineteenth century, but only became reality when work started in the 1990s. The link, which opened in 2000, is a mixture of an 8-km (5-mile) long bridge, a 4-km (2.5-mile) artificial island and a 4-km (2.5-mile) long tunnel. It has two levels, with a road on the upper deck and a railway line beneath.

▲ The spectacular Öresund Link spans the 14-km (9-mile) strait between Malmö and Copenhagen.

TRANSPORT BY WATER

Ferries provide sea links with many countries including the UK, Germany, Denmark, Finland, Estonia and Poland. Stockholm, Malmö and Göteborg are all major ports. Sweden also has an extensive network of canals, most famously the Göta Canal, which was built in the nineteenth century to connect Sweden's west coast with the Baltic Sea. The canal extends some 579 km (360 miles) from Göteborg in the west, linking lakes Vänern and Vättern. It was originally used for transporting timber and iron, but today is an extremely popular tourist attraction.

COMMUNICATIONS

Sweden is a world leader in communications and information technology, and this is reflected in the number of mobile phones and use of the Internet among Swedes generally. According to Telekom Online, Sweden has more mobile phones than it has people – 10 million phones for a population of 9 million people. This does not mean, however, that every person in Sweden owns a mobile phone, just that many people own more than one phone. In 2005, Sweden became the first country in the world to introduce a secure system of electronic identification using mobile phones. Called e-ID, this system will allow people to access their bank accounts and other secure information via their phones.

An extremely high proportion of people in Sweden use the Internet – 75.6 per cent in 2005 compared with 63 per cent for the USA and 62.8 per cent in the UK. Many Swedes use the Internet regularly for transactions such as shopping, looking for jobs, reading online newspapers and booking tickets. Government agencies, such as county and municipal councils and the tax board, also have highly developed

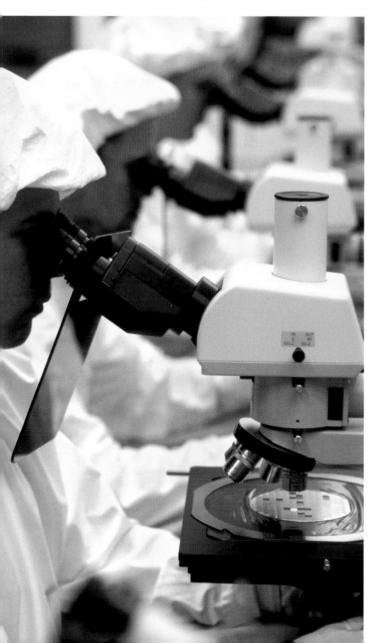

◀ People making electronic wafers in a Stockholm laboratory owned by Ericsson, the Swedish electronics and communications company.

websites, allowing people to contact them via the Internet and, for example, to submit their tax returns online.

MEDIA

Until 1987, the Swedish national public service broadcaster, Sveriges Television (SVT), provided the only television channels available in the country. Since that date many commercial channels have been introduced, some of which are available only via cable or satellite. The next big change will be in 2008, when analogue television transmissions will end. From that date, all television sets must be converted to digital, either through a set-top box or through cable or satellite connections. Sweden will be one of the first countries in Europe to make this switch-over.

Newspapers and magazines are very popular in Sweden – around 90 per cent of adults read a newspaper every day, and many of them have a newspaper delivered to their home in the morning. The most popular national papers include *Dagens Nyheter* (The Daily News) and *Göteborgs-Posten* (The Göteborg Post). There are also evening newspapers (published around noon every day), and many smaller newspapers which target a local readership. Sweden was also the original home of *Metro*, which was launched in 1995 in Stockholm. This free newspaper is now distributed to commuters, office workers and shoppers in 88 major cities around the world, and reaches a readership of 18.5 million people every day.

► The Kaknäs Television Tower in Stockholm rises 155 m (508 ft), and is the tallest structure in Scandinavia. It is the centre for radio and television broadcasts across Sweden.

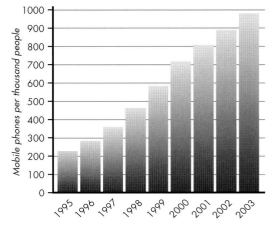

▲ Mobile phone use, 1995-2003

Did you know?

Swedish ports handled more than 167 million tonnes (164,362,490 tons) of goods in 2004.

CHAPTER 10

Education and Health

Sweden has extremely high standards of education and healthcare. The Swedes allocate 7.7 per cent of GDP to education, and 9.2 per cent of GDP to healthcare, which puts them among the top spenders in these areas in the developed world. Sweden has one of the highest literacy rates in the world (100 per cent).

EARLY EDUCATION

There is an extensive system of early learning and childcare to look after children before they start school (see page 33). However, children in Sweden start their compulsory schooling relatively late compared with many other developed countries. Children must attend school from the ages of seven to 16, but a pre-school place is allocated to every child who is six years of age, if their parents wish them to attend at this age. The school year starts in mid to late August and finishes in mid June, with a holiday over the Christmas and New Year period. Most children go to the school that is nearest to their home. Education is free, including school meals, transport to and from school, and equipment and books. There are a few independent schools, which often offer a different specialization from the state schools, for example, sports or music.

HIGHER EDUCATION AND BEYOND

The vast majority, about 98 per cent, of Swedish students continue on to upper secondary school, which is also free. Students can choose subjects from 17 national programmes, including both academic and vocational components, which they study for three years. Many continue their studies at university, or at specialized training colleges such as teacher training or healthcare training. Higher education tuition is free, and students can apply for government grants and loans to help with their living expenses. There are universities in all of Sweden's major cities – Stockholm, Göteborg, Uppsala and Lund – for example, as well as specialized institutions such

◀ Children at work during a question and answer session at school.

as the Karolinska Institute (medicine) and the Luleå University of Technology. There are also several private higher education institutions, including the Stockholm School of Economics and the Chalmers University of Technology.

Continued learning in adulthood is considered important in Sweden. Many people take courses at one of the 147 'folk high schools' around the country. Adult learning is financed by government grants, and municipalities are obliged by law to provide education for adults, to give adult learners the skills needed 'to take part in social and working life'. Similarly, municipalities must provide language classes for immigrants to learn and improve their basic Swedish.

Education and health

- Life expectancy at birth male: 77.9
- Life expectancy at birth female: 82.4
- Infant mortality rate per 1,000: 3
- Under five mortality rate per 1,000: 3
- Physicians per 1,000 people: 3
- Health expenditure as % of GDP: 9.2%
- Education expenditure as % of GDP: 7.7%
- Primary net enrolment: 100%
- Pupil-teacher ratio, primary: 11.2
- Adult literacy as % age 15+: near 100%

Source: United Nations Agencies and World Bank

Focus on: Sami schools

Children from Sami families in northern Sweden may, if they wish, attend Sami school. There are Sami schools in Karesuando, Lannavaara, Kiruna, Gällivare, Jokkmokk and Tärnaby. These schools are funded by the state, and take students between the ages of seven and 12. Children are taught in the Sami language as well as Swedish, and the curriculum covers Sami culture and issues together with the subjects taught in other municipal schools. The schools are run by the Sami School Board, which is overseen by the Sami Parliament (see page 25).

◀ University students wear their white graduation caps as they rush out to meet friends and relatives after their graduation ceremony in Uppsala in 2003.

Sweden has one of the lowest infant mortality rates (the number of babies who die at birth) in the world, at 3 per 1,000 births, and one of the highest life expectancies, at 77.9 years for men and 82.4 years for women. It has an efficient health service, which is completely free for people up to the age of 20.

PAYING FOR HEALTHCARE

Sweden's healthcare is run by the county councils (see page 24). The health system is financed through contributions made by employers and an income tax that is set by individual county councils. In addition, patients pay a charge when they consult a doctor, but once they have paid a certain amount (SEK 900, about £66 or US$123) in a 12-month period, treatment is free. Similarly, patients must pay for medicines up to a certain amount, but after that they are subsidized.

A major issue in Sweden is the high rate of absence from work through sickness, often as a result of stress-related problems. The average annual number of days off work because of illness has risen rapidly from 17 in 1995 to 32 in 2002. In 1993, the government changed the rules so that employees would lose their pay for the first day taken off work. However, after this initial 'qualifying day', employees receive about 80 per cent of their salary while they are off work, and many people attribute the high levels of sick leave at least partly to the generous government-funded provision. The government is trying to encourage people to work, even on a part-time basis. In 2003, the cost of sick leave payments came to SEK 110 billion (£8 billion or US$15 billion).

In general, Sweden's population has been growing steadily

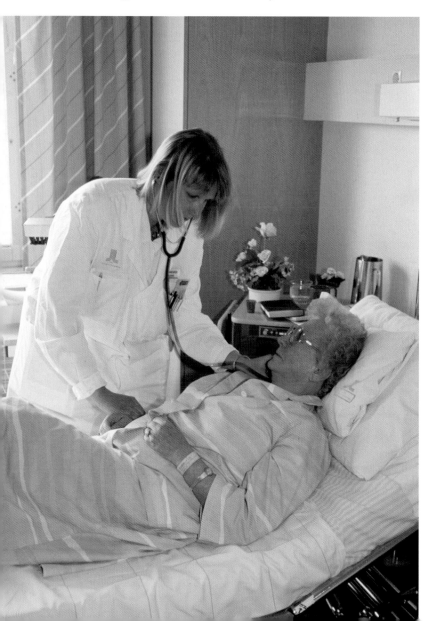

◀ A doctor examines an elderly patient at a hospital in Stockholm. Healthcare is of a very high standard in Sweden.

healthier since the 1930s. Issues for the future include an increasing number of people with allergies, and problems with obesity, particularly in young people. According to a study by Karolinska University Hospital, the number of obese seven-year-olds in Stockholm has increased from 8.5 per cent to 21 per cent since 1990. Experts blame a mixture of the increased popularity of fast foods and fizzy drinks and more hours spent in front of the television and computer screen. This is despite Sweden's nationwide sport programmes aimed at children, and the fact that commercials aimed at under-12s are banned on Swedish television.

Focus on: Winter Swedes

During the dark days of winter, people in northern Sweden experience 24-hour darkness (see page 15), while even in the south days are short and cold. Many Swedes travel abroad during the winter holidays to find the sun. Destinations such as Thailand and Sri Lanka are popular, as shown by the number of Swedish deaths when a giant tsunami devastated coastlines around the Indian Ocean in 2004. More than 500 Swedes were killed in the disaster – the highest number for any European nation.

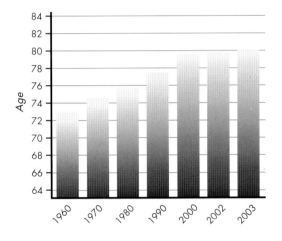

▲ Life expectancy at birth, 1960-2003

▼ For Swedish people, the festival of St Lucia (see page 49), held in December, brightens up the long, dark days of winter.

CHAPTER 11

Culture and Religion

Sweden occupies a central place in European cultural tradition, and has given the world many writers, musicians, actors and artists of renown, including the playwright August Strindberg, the pop group ABBA, the actress Greta Garbo, the filmmaker Ingmar Bergman and the artist Carl Larsson.

LANGUAGE

Although Swedish is the main language of Sweden, it is not by law the country's official language. In 2005, a proposal to formalize the status of Swedish was narrowly rejected by the Swedish parliament. Nevertheless, the Swedes are very proud of their language, which is related to Danish and Norwegian, and it is the principal tongue spoken in Sweden. Most Swedes also speak at least one other language, usually English, but French, German and Spanish are also popular. Sweden has five official minority languages: Sami (Lapp), Finnish, Meänkieli (Tornedalen Finnish), Yiddish and Romani Chib (a Gypsy language). In recent years, a variety of Swedish has emerged from city suburbs that have large immigrant populations. This new language is a mixture of Swedish and words taken from the immigrants' home languages and is known as Rinkeby Swedish, after a suburb of Stockholm. Rinkeby Swedish varies according to the background and location of the people speaking it.

FOOD

In the days before refrigeration, the storage of food was vitally important for survival through the long winter months in Sweden. The summer harvest of fruits and vegetables was preserved and pickled, and meat and fish were

◀ This painting by the Swedish artist, Carl Larsson (1853-1919), was one of a series he made of his home in Sundborn. Larsson's work became hugely popular in Sweden and beyond.

smoked, salted or dried for storage. Today, modern methods of food storage have made such measures unnecessary, but the traditional tastes of Swedish food and the importance of seasonal produce remain very important. People still go out into the forests and wild places of Sweden to pick berries and mushrooms (see page 17), and crayfish and fermented herring are national delicacies that are still valued and enjoyed.

The best known Swedish meal is probably *smörgåsbord* – a buffet of many types of delicious food, including open sandwiches and savouries, from which people help themselves.

? Did you know?

'Ombudsman' is a word that has come direct from the Swedish language into English. It means a person who works as an official, monitoring public agencies and investigating complaints made by members of the public.

Focus on: Runes

Runes are an ancient form of writing used in Sweden and other northern European countries. The runic alphabet takes its name from its first six letters 'Futhark' (the 't' and the 'h' are one letter), and was developed by early Germanic peoples. More than 3,000 stones inscribed with runic messages have been found in Sweden, many in the region around Uppsala. These stones were usually memorials to the dead. The runes were cut into the stone, then carefully painted, often in red, to make them more visible.

▼ The Swedish pop group ABBA came to fame after winning the Eurovision Song Contest in 1974, and went on to become one of the most successful pop groups of all time.

THE ARTS

All aspects of the arts play an important part in Swedish life. Large amounts of public money are spent in subsidies to support cultural and artistic activities with the aim of making them available to everyone. The Swedish government funds some major institutions directly, for example, the Royal Opera and the Royal Dramatic Theatre. Municipal and county councils allocate funds to museums, libraries, local theatres, orchestras, and opera and dance companies. Sweden's vibrant artistic, literary and musical tradition continues to produce talents such as the film director, Lukas Moodysson, and the author, Per Olov Enquist.

RELIGION IN SWEDEN

Until 2000, when the link between church and state was broken, the national church of Sweden was the Lutheran Church. Before that, a child born to a parent who belonged to the Church of Sweden automatically became a member. Now it is up to parents to decide whether or not to have their children baptized. Other Christian churches also have a presence in Sweden, notably the Roman Catholic Church, the Pentecostal and various Baptist churches. As a result of immigration into Sweden, the Muslim population has increased rapidly to between 300,000 and 350,000 in 2004, and there are mosques being built in several places. There is a small Jewish population of about 18,000 people.

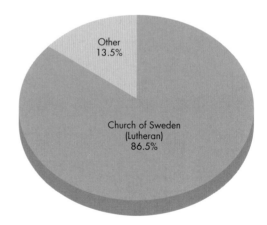

▲ Major religions

? Did you know?

The festival of Walpurgis is named after Saint Walburga, who was born in England in 710.

◀ A sculpture appears out of the waters of the Norrström in Strömmen, Stockholm, with the Royal Opera House in the background.

FESTIVALS

Many of Sweden's major festivals are based around the Christian calendar, for example, Advent, Christmas and Easter. Christmas is celebrated mainly on Christmas Eve, when children are given presents. At Easter, children dress up as witches in honour of an old story telling how witches traditionally meet up with the devil at Easter. Other popular festivals are St Lucia, Walpurgis and Midsummer's Day. St Lucia takes place on 13 December and is celebrated across Sweden with 'Lucia processions' led by a young girl dressed in white and wearing a special Lucia crown with (battery powered) candles. This festival of light brightens up a dark time of year and is a national holiday. Walpurgis, on 30 April, dates back to Viking times. It is a celebration of the end of winter and the coming of spring, and is marked by the lighting of huge bonfires across the country. Midsummer is also an old pagan festival, celebrating the longest day of the year. Families and friends meet up to eat herring and potatoes, and in many places people dance around a maypole.

Focus on: Strindberg

August Strindberg (1849-1912), Sweden's most famous writer and playwright, was born in Stockholm. His realistic and often satirical style of writing about people and situations shocked theatre audiences and readers of his stories and novels alike. His novel, *The Red Room* (1879), made him famous, as did plays such as *The Father* (1887) and *Miss Julie* (1888). Strindberg was married three times, and had difficult and complicated relationships with women throughout his life. In his later years, he experimented with new forms of writing for the stage in works such as *The Dance of Death* (1901).

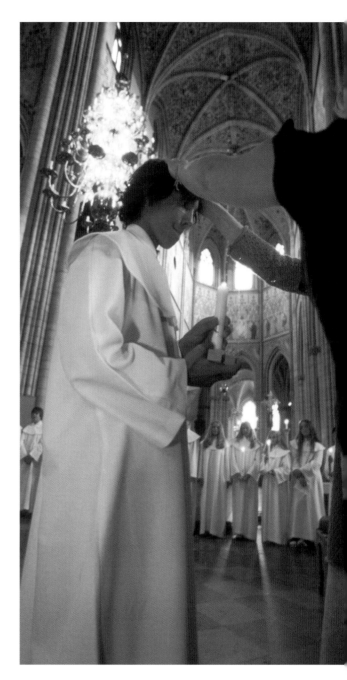

▲ Boys and girls at a confirmation service in Uppsala Cathedral. The boy is being blessed after receiving a confirmation candle.

CHAPTER 12

Leisure and Tourism

Outdoor sports and recreation are hugely important pastimes in Sweden. The country's sparse population and dramatic and varied scenery mean that outdoor activities have become an integral part of the lifestyle of most Swedes. Hiking, ice hockey, running, downhill and cross-country skiing, sailing, canoeing, cycling, long distance ice-skating, fishing, golf, football and tennis are all immensely popular.

TRAILS

Sweden is crisscrossed with long distance trails for cyclists and hikers. For example, the Sverigeleden bike trail runs the length of Sweden, from Helsingborg in the south to Karesuando in the far north, a distance of 2,590 km (1,609 miles). Cycling is also very popular on the large islands of Gotland and Öland. Several of Sweden's most popular hiking trails start on the edge of its big cities, for example, the Sörmlandsleden, an 850-km (528-mile) trail, starts on the outskirts of Stockholm. There are many spectacular mountain trails. The best known is the Kungsleden in northern Norrland. Hikers can stay in mountain stations and cabins, which offer food and accommodation along the way. In the winter, ski trails are marked with red poles for cross-country skiing, and people flock to downhill ski resorts such as Åre and Sälen.

SPORTING HEROES

The Swedish enthusiasm for active pursuits may explain why so many Swedish sportsmen

▼ A hiker sits on a rock above the Rapa River valley in Sarek National Park.

and women have been successful on the world stage. The Swedish tennis legend, Björn Borg, inspired many of his fellow Swedes to take up tennis, including players such as Stefan Edberg and Mats Wilander. Alpine (downhill) skiing has seen national heroes such as the *slalom* specialist, Ingemar Stenmark, and the Olympic medallist (in 1992 and 1994), Pernilla Wiberg. Football is a popular sport in Sweden, and fans follow their local teams and the national team.

The best known Swedish footballer is Fredrik (Freddie) Ljungberg, who was voted Swedish Midfielder of the Year in 2004, although he currently plays for a British club (Arsenal) rather than a Swedish one.

Did you know?

By the time he retired in 1983, tennis player Björn Borg had won 62 men's singles titles.

Focus on: Vasaloppet

This famous Swedish cross-country ski race has its origins in the events of 1520, when Gustav Vasa (see page 11) tried unsuccessfully to persuade the residents of Dalarna in central Sweden to rise up against Danish rule. Vasa was forced to flee, closely pursued by Danish troops. However, the people of Dalarna changed their minds and sent their fastest skiers to catch up with Vasa, which they did at Sälen. Today, the race runs in the opposite direction to Vasa's original journey, starting in Sälen and ending 90 km (56 miles) away in Mora, which is where Vasa's army eventually defeated the Danes. Since 1922, the cross-country ski race has been held annually on the first Sunday in March (with a few cancellations because of mild winters). In 2005 it attracted more than 15,000 skiers. The record for the gruelling course is a remarkable 3 hours, 38 minutes and 57 seconds.

◀ Christian Olsson of Sweden on his way to victory in the men's triple jump during the Golden League athletics meeting at Rome's Olympic Stadium in July 2004.

TOURISM

The Swedes make the most of their country and its attractions, but they also love to travel abroad. Favourite destinations include Thailand, the USA, Egypt, Australia and the Canary Islands. Tourism into Sweden has increased dramatically since the 1970s. Many people come for 'nature tourism', attracted by Sweden's expanses of unspoilt wilderness and the chance to play some golf or do some fishing or take part in more extreme sports, such as mountain biking or sea kayaking. Lappland, in the far north, is a major draw for tourists. In the winter months, people come to view the magnificent Aurora Borealis (Northern Lights), which fills the night sky with dramatic forms in greens, violets and reds. There is also the opportunity to learn about Sami life, and try out activities such as dog-sledding or snow-mobiling. At Jukkasjärvi, near Kiruna, tourists can stay in a hotel made entirely of ice. The walls and even the beds are chipped out of solid blocks of ice, and guests sleep on thick reindeer skins to keep out the cold.

SWEDISH CITIES

In recent years, Swedish cities have witnessed the biggest growth in tourism. Stockholm, Göteborg and Malmö all have different attractions for the visitor. Stockholm is renowned for its beautiful location, and is also home to Sweden's Royal Palace and major

Tourism in Sweden

- Tourist arrivals, millions: 7.627
- Earnings from tourism in US$: 6,547,999,744
- Tourism as % foreign earnings: 4.9
- Tourist departures, millions: 12.579
- Expenditure on tourism in US$: 9,374,999,552

Source: World Bank

Focus on: Jokkmokk winter market

Every year in February, the northern town of Jokkmokk comes alive as it holds its famous winter market. This is a Sami celebration, and it started in 1605 when King Karl IX decreed that marketplaces should be established in northern Sweden. Jokkmokk developed on the site of a Sami winter camp, and the market quickly became an important meeting place for the Sami people. Today, the market is still a major Sami festival, with stalls selling Sami handicrafts and performances of Sami music. The week long market attracts thousands of visitors – 80,000 in 2005 – from all parts of the world.

◀ This satellite image shows the Aurora Borealis over Norway and Sweden.

museums such as the National Museum of Fine Arts. One of the most fascinating museums, and a major tourist attraction since it opened in 1990, is the Vasamuseet (Vasa Museum). The warship *Vasa* capsized in Stockholm harbour in 1628. More than 300 years later it was discovered and salvaged and, following years of painstaking conservation and restoration work, it opened to the public. The *Vasa* is the only intact seventeenth-century warship in the world, and the museum is the most visited in the whole of Scandinavia.

Göteborg, Sweden's second biggest city, boasts Liseberg, Scandinavia's largest amusement park. It also offers a wide variety of festivals and events throughout the year. Malmö has a

famous summer festival, which attracts more than one million visitors. Malmö is also exploiting the new possibilities opened up by the Öresund Link (see page 39), which have connected the city more closely with Copenhagen in Denmark.

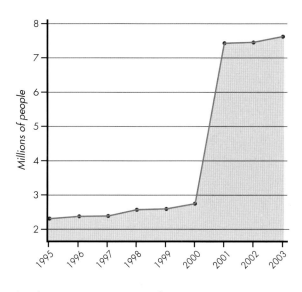

▲ Changes in international tourism, 1995-2003

? Did you know?

Lappland has one hundred days of midnight sun a year.

▶ The Ice Hotel in Jukkasjärvi is made every year from the crystal-clear frozen waters of the Torne River.

CHAPTER 13

Environment and Conservation

The Swedes have a deep-rooted respect for their land. From ancient times, there has been a tradition of Allemansrätt – the 'Right of Common Access' – which allows people to roam the countryside freely and camp anywhere, so long as they do not damage crops or invade other people's privacy. People may also pick wild produce such as berries and mushrooms.

NATIONAL PARKS

Sweden was the first country in Europe to set up national parks to protect its country's natural environments. The first nine national parks were founded in 1909, and today there are 28. Together with nature reserves and other special areas, about 8 per cent of Sweden's land area is protected. In some parks, camping and lighting fires is not permitted but the right to roam freely and collect wild produce still applies. A large area (about 90 per cent) of Sweden's national parks is mountainous, but other environments also include swamps, forests and archipelago landscapes like those in Ängsö National Park on the east coast. The largest parks are Stora Sjöfallet, Sarek and Padjelanta in the far north, all of which have dramatic mountain scenery. Sarek has large expanses of true mountain wilderness, without any trails or facilities for visitors.

WILDLIFE

The wilderness areas of northern Sweden provide habitats for a large variety of animals and plants. Animal life in these areas includes wolves, wolverines, lynx, arctic foxes and bears. There are also many beavers, red deer, elk and reindeer. One of Sweden's newest national parks, Färnebofjärden in central Sweden, is a rich mixture of river, water meadows and ancient forest which houses more than 100 different

◀ Researchers collect data from a tranquillized bear in Dalarna in 2001.

species of bird, including woodpeckers and owls. Another national park, Abisko in the far north, is home to the rare Lapp orchid, and is the only place in Sweden where this plant grows.

PROTECTING THE ENVIRONMENT

Sweden was one of the first European countries to address the problems of industrial emissions. In 1967, the Swedish government established the Swedish Environmental Protection Agency and two years later it passed the Environment Protection Act, designed to reduce and control emissions from all types of industry. The act dramatically reduced emissions into the air and water from Swedish industry, but Sweden continues to suffer from airborne emissions from other countries over which it has little or no control. In 1999, a new Environmental Code became law. It covers all activities that may harm the environment, regardless of whether they are carried out by companies or individuals. The code allows tougher measures than ever before against those who break the law, including fines and imprisonment.

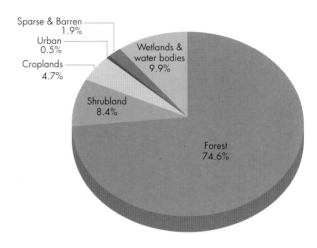

▲ Habitat type as percentage of total area

Focus on: Linnaeus

Carl Linnaeus (also called von Linné) (1707-78) was born on a farm in southern Sweden and from a young age was fascinated with the plant life around him. He studied botany (the science of plants) at Lund and Uppsala universities, and in the 1730s travelled to Lappland to study the plant life there. He is celebrated as the scientist who devised the system of classifying plants and animals with two Latin names (for example, *Primula vulgaris*, which means 'common primrose'). This system of classification is still used today.

▲ A statue of Carl Linnaeus stands in front of the central station in Stockholm.

ENVIRONMENTAL PROBLEMS

While Sweden has cleaned up its industries and tackled the problems of emissions, environmental problems such as acid rain, air and water pollution and greenhouse gases still remain. Acid rain poisons lakes and other waterways. It is still a problem in Sweden, particularly in the south, although the situation is far better than it was in the 1960s, before controls were introduced.

The majority (80 per cent) of greenhouse gases come from energy production and transportation. The number of vehicles in Sweden continues to increase every year, and the vast majority of these vehicles burn the fossil fuels petrol and diesel. However, Sweden is encouraging the use of cleaner fuels such as ethanol, natural gas and biogas, and sales of vehicles running on these fuels are some of the highest in Europe. Other schemes to promote sustainable transport include joint ownership of pools of cars that can be shared by communities, and tax incentives to encourage people to drive cars that run on 'clean' fuels. In 2006, despite opposition from residents, Stockholm ran a trial for congestion charging. This involved making motorists pay a toll to use roads in the centre of the city.

THE BALTIC SEA

Water pollution is a particular issue in the Baltic Sea, and Sweden is working very closely with its Baltic region neighbours to address the problem. Discharges from shipping and from countries around the Baltic are causing large areas of the sea to become lifeless in a process called eutrophication. In 1996, Sweden was one of the founder members of Baltic 21, a regional organization that is focusing on the sustainable development of the Baltic Sea.

◀ Swedish Rail is one of the largest users of 'green' electricity in Europe. Since 1999, all of their electric trains have been powered by electricity from renewable sources – either hydro, wind or biofuels.

Environmental and conservation data

📂 Forested area as % total land area: 74.6

📂 Protected area as % total land area: 7.2

📂 Number of protected areas: 3,946

SPECIES DIVERSITY

Category	Known species	Threatened species
Mammals	60	7
Breeding birds	259	2
Reptiles	7	n/a
Amphibians	13	n/a
Fish	78	n/a
Plants	1,750	3

Source: World Resources Institute

Focus on: Recycling

Sweden has the highest rate of recycling in Europe. Commercial and domestic waste is sorted and recycled in various ways. People sort their plastic, glass, metal, paper and newspapers and take bigger items, such as electrical appliances or furniture, to waste recycling centres. By law, any company that sells certain categories of product (for example, packaging, tyres, paper and electronic goods) in Sweden is also responsible for the collection of that product and the cost of its recycling at the end its life. This legislation has made companies think very carefully about the materials they use in their products and packaging.

▲ Cycling is very popular in Stockholm and helps to reduce air pollution in the city.

CHAPTER 14

Future Challenges

Sweden seems well equipped to face the challenges of the twenty-first century. The country boasts a culture of equality and a strong respect for freedom of speech and democracy.

A MULTICULTURAL SOCIETY

Since the 1950s, Swedes have adjusted to the fact that their country has become increasingly multicultural. During the 1990s, attacks on ethnic minorities by racist groups outraged the vast majority of Swedes, who are passionately opposed to any form of racism. The Swedish government has worked hard to tackle these problems. In 2001 it presented a national action plan to combat racism and discrimination in all areas, and an active integration policy to give 'equal rights, responsibilities and opportunities for all, irrespective of ethnic and cultural background'. Nevertheless, disparities between different sections of the population remain. The government is therefore embarking on various projects to try to improve education and employment prospects for people from immigrant communities, for example, by providing better training in Swedish and the increased recognition of professional qualifications that have been gained abroad rather than in Sweden.

THE EUROPEAN UNION

Since becoming a member of the EU in 1995, Sweden has worked hard to promote the issues it considers important. These include enlargement (see page 36), greater openness in government, reducing unemployment and tackling environmental problems. Most Swedes value their membership of the EU and regard it as a way of working more closely with their European neighbours over issues such as reducing emissions that cause acid rain and dealing with the problems of pollution in the Baltic Sea. The environment is a high priority for most Swedes, and the country has clear goals and strategies for tackling future environmental problems (see box opposite).

◀ Swedish Muslims pray at a mosque in central Stockholm. Sweden's future is as a multicultural society.

THE ECONOMY

Since the crisis of the early 1990s, the Swedish economy has recovered remarkably well and prospects are good for the future. While the economy relies very heavily on exports, there has been a shift in the type of export from traditional products, such as steel and timber, to sectors such as IT and telecommunications. Sweden's reliance on exports makes it vulnerable to changes in the worldwide economy and challenges from emerging economic powers such as China and India. Nevertheless, Sweden's vigorous tradition of research and development places many of its companies at the cutting edge in areas such as IT, and the future seems bright for Sweden's economy and for the Swedish people in the twenty-first century.

Focus on: The environment

The Swedish government has produced a bill that lists 15 general targets relating to the environment, which it plans to achieve by 2020-25:
1. Reduced climate impact
2. Clean air
3. Natural acidification only (zero acid rain)
4. A non-toxic environment
5. A protective ozone layer
6. A safe radiation environment
7. Zero eutrophication (water pollution)
8. Flourishing lakes and streams
9. Good-quality groundwater
10. A balanced marine environment, flourishing coastal areas and archipelagos
11. Thriving wetlands
12. Sustainable forests
13. A varied agricultural landscape
14. A magnificent mountain landscape
15. A good built environment (for example, in cities)

► This futuristic sculpture, designed in 1974 by Edvin Öhrström and known as the Glass Obelisk, is an example of the mix of traditional materials and modern design for which Sweden is famous. The 37-metre (121-ft) glass pillar stands in Sergels Torg, a large public square in the centre of Stockholm.

Timeline

c.15,000 BC Ice covers Sweden.

c.12,000 BC The earliest known human habitation in Sweden.

c.1800 BC Bronze weapons and other objects become widespread.

By c. 1500 BC Trade routes established as far south as the River Danube.

c.500 BC Iron working begins.

AD 800 Viking people from southern Scandinavia start to raid and conquer lands overseas.

829 Christianity arrives in Sweden with the missionary Ansgar.

1008 Olof Skötkonung is the first Swedish king to be baptized.

1200s Trading towns such as Visby become important centres for the Hanseatic League.

1350 The bubonic plague devastates the Swedish population.

1397 The Kalmar Union unites Sweden, Norway and Denmark.

1415 Sweden completes conquest of Finland.

1520 The 'Stockholm bloodbath' – 80 leading Swedish noblemen are executed in Stockholm.

1521 The Kalmar Union comes to an end.

1523 Gustav Vasa elected king of Sweden.

1544 Vasa makes the monarchy hereditary and adopts Lutheranism as the state religion.

1560s-1650s Sweden builds a Baltic Empire.

1611-32 The reign of military genius King Gustav II Adolf.

1618-48 The Thirty Years' War.

1654 The abdication of Queen Kristina brings Vasa dynasty to an end.

1735 Carl Linnaeus publishes *Systema Naturae*, his classification of living things.

1810 Napoleon's marshal, Jean Baptiste Bernadotte, is elected to be Swedish king.

1812 Beginning of policy of neutrality.

1814 After a short war, Norway becomes part of Sweden.

1850s-1930 Almost 1.5 million Swedes emigrate.

1867-8 Famine devastates Sweden.

1901 First Nobel prizes awarded.

1905 Norway gains independence from Sweden.

1914-18 Sweden remains neutral during the First World War.

1921 Swedish women receive the vote.

1939-45 Sweden remains neutral during the Second World War.

1946 Sweden becomes a member of the United Nations.

1950s Start of immigration into Sweden.

1953-61 Swedish diplomat Dag Hammarskjöld is secretary-general of the United Nations.

1986 Assassination of the Swedish prime minister, Olof Palme.

1993 First Sami Parliament in Kiruna.

1995 Sweden becomes a member of the European Union.

2000 Opening of the Öresund Link between Malmö and Copenhagen; connection between state and religion is broken as Lutheran Church is no longer the national church of Sweden.

2003 Assassination of Foreign Minister Anna Lindh in Stockholm.

2003 Swedes reject the Euro.

2004 More than 500 Swedes are killed by a tsunami that devastates coastlines around the Indian Ocean.

2006 A row over the closure of a website that has featured images of the Prophet Muhammad leads to the resignation of Foreign Minister Laila Freivalds.

Glossary

Acid rain A form of pollution caused by sulphur dioxide and nitrogen dioxide emissions, which dissolve in rainfall.

Archaeologist Someone who studies the remains of ancient peoples.

Archipelago A group of islands.

Armaments Weapons and other military equipment.

Asylum seekers People who seek refuge in a country to escape persecution in their home country.

Aurora Borealis A phenomenon in the atmosphere around the North Pole that is caused by the interaction of the earth's magnetic field and charged particles from the sun.

Baptist Church A Christian church that believes in adult baptism by total immersion in water.

Biofuels Fuels that are produced from organic matter.

Byzantine Empire The eastern part of the Roman Empire, which continued after the fall of the western Roman Empire until the capture of its capital, Constantinople, in 1453.

Cold War The state of political hostility between the two superpowers, the USA and the Soviet Union, that started after the end of the Second World War and ended with the break-up of the Soviet Union in 1991.

Consensus General agreement.

Constitution An agreed set of rules and laws according to which a state or organization is governed.

Democracy A political system in which representatives are chosen by the people in free elections.

Dynasty A series of rulers from the same family who succeed one another in power.

Egalitarian Believing in the principle that all people are equal and deserve equal rights and opportunities.

Emissions Waste gases and particles given out from industry or from vehicle exhausts.

Entrepreneur A business person who is willing to take on financial risks in pursuit of profit.

Eutrophication A process of pollution by which nutrients are carried off agricultural land into the sea. The nutrients feed algae which then grow rapidly, depriving other sea life of oxygen and light.

Formalize To make formal or official.

Fossil fuels Types of energy sources, such as oil, coal and gas, that are formed by fossilized plants and animals. They release carbon when they are burned.

Geothermal energy Energy that is tapped from deep below the earth's surface.

Globalization The process by which trade and business is increasingly conducted at a global scale.

Greenhouse gases Gases such as carbon dioxide and ozone, which play a major role in global warming.

Gross Domestic Product (GDP) The total value of goods and services produced within the borders of a country.

Hanseatic League (Hansa) An alliance of trading cities in northern Europe between the thirteenth and the seventeenth centuries.

Hierarchical Describes something arranged in a graded order.

Hydro-electric power The production of electricity by harnessing the power of moving water.

Industrialization The process of developing factories and manufacturing on a large scale.

Lutheran Church A Protestant Christian church committed to the principles set out by the sixteenth-century reformer, Martin Luther.

Missionary Someone who travels to places to convert people to his or her religion.

Norse An ancient Scandinavian language and culture.

Racism Abuse towards people on the grounds of their race, or ethnic origin.

Recession A time of depression (slump) in economic activity.

Referendum A national vote on a single issue.

Reformation The movement in the sixteenth century that challenged the power of the Roman Catholic Church and led to the formation of the Protestant churches.

Rune An ancient form of writing used in Scandinavia.

Satirical Describes something that ridicules or points out absurdities, for example, a satirical cartoon or piece of writing.

Scandinavia The northern European countries of Sweden, Norway and Denmark.

Subsidy Money paid by a government to support a particular concern, usually for the public good.

Trade union An organization that represents the rights of the workers in discussion with employers.

Tsunami A giant sea surge caused by an earthquake under the ocean.

Further Information

BOOKS TO READ

Countries of the World – Sweden
Leif Schack-Nielsen
(Evans Brothers, 2005)

Eyewitness Travel Guides– Sweden
Ulf Johansson, Forlag Streiffert
(Dorling Kindersley, 2005)

Insight Guides – Sweden
 Jane Hutchings
(APA Publications, 1999)

Nations of the World – Sweden
Robbie Butler
(Raintree, 2003)

Raoul Wallenberg
Sharon Linnea
(Jewish Publication Society of America, 1994)

The Royal Diaries: Kristina, the Girl King, Sweden, 1638
Carolyn Meyer
(Scholastic, 2003)

And the Wolves Howled: Fragments of Two Lifetimes
Barbro Karlen, Julie Martin (translator)
(Clairview Books, 2000)

Burned Child Seeks the Fire: A Memoir
Cordelia Edvardson
(Beacon Press, 1997)

Carl and Karin Larsson: Creators of the Swedish Style
Elisabet Hidemark
(Bullfinch Press, 2001)

FICTION

Pippi Longstocking
Astrid Lindgren
(Puffin, 2005)

The Summer Book
Tove Jansson, Esther Freud (translator)
(Sort of Books, 2003)

Swedish Folk Tales
Polly Lawson (editor)
(Floris Books, 2004)

USEFUL WEBSITES

http://www.sweden.se
The official website for Sweden, with articles and information about all aspects of the country.

http://www.royalcourt.se
The official website for the Swedish monarchy.

http://www.sweden.gov.se
The Swedish government website.

http://www.internat.naturvardsverket.se
Website for the Swedish Environmental Protection Agency.

http://www.sametinget.se
Website for the Sami Parliament.

http://www.baltic21.org/index.php
Information about Baltic 21 (see page 56).

Index

About the Author

Nicola Barber is the author of many children's non-fiction books. specializing in geography, history and the arts.